The Retirement Compass

NAVIGATING THE RETIREMENT STORM

Rick Clark
& Megan Clark

Clark Financial Solutions

RESTON, VIRGINIA

Rick Clark
Clark Financial Solutions
1984 Isaac Newton Sq. West
Ste. 203
Reston, VA 20190
www.clarkfinancialplanning.com

Book layout ©2013 BookDesignTemplates.com

The Retirement Compass/ Rick Clark & Megan Clark. —1st ed.
ISBN 978-1978439481

Contents

I would like to dedicate this book to the 700-plus families who have entrusted us with their livelihoods, their life's savings, their dreams, and their financial well-being.

In the long run, we shape our lives, and we shape ourselves. The process never ends until we die. And the choices we make are ultimately our own responsibility.

—ELEANOR ROOSEVELT

Foreword

My name is Megan Clark. I'm Rick Clark's daughter and, proudly, the CEO at Clark & Associates Inc. Financial Solutions, the firm he founded in 1987. I thought I would start by sharing with you some of the lessons I've learned from my father. They may seem pretty basic, but they make a huge difference in the way I live my life.

1. If you fall, get up. If you fall again, get up again.
2. Treat others the way you want to be treated.
3. Work hard, play hard.
4. If you are going to do something half-assed, then don't bother doing it at all.

My father consistently instilled in me the idea that you can be whatever you dream as long as you work hard enough for it, and nothing worth doing is ever easy. Raised by Depression-era parents in a family of five kids, his father was a World War II veteran and an electrical engineer.

My dad didn't have all that much growing up, so he learned to work for what he wanted and needed. I think he has had more jobs than any other 10 people combined. He has milked cows, worked as an auto mechanic, been a pilot. Now, as a skilled senior advisor in the financial planning industry, he has proved the American dream still exists ... if you are willing to put in the blood, the sweat and the tears.

As a soccer player, when I fell, I could always hear my dad yell, "Get up, you are fine." I learned from the experience, or, as he would say, I learned to move on. To this day, he believes every disappointment is an opportunity to get better and to be better.

I can't think of a more vital lesson for a parent to pass on to their child.

Recently I read a post from Simon Sinek, the author of "Start With Why," that reinforced the valuable message my dad always taught me: "The primary ingredient for progress is optimism. The unwavering belief that something can be better drives the human race forward."

My dad always seems to have been driven to help others. When I was growing up, he always was serving. Whether it was assisting in building a neighbor's deck or plowing someone's snow-covered driveway, he was always the first to offer help.

Dad is a giver who wears his heart on his sleeve. I am so grateful for that. Growing up, we had "golden rules" posted around our house, and I will never forget "treat others the way you want to be treated." This single notion is the reason my father founded Clark Financial Solutions, and it's the reason you are holding this book in your hands. Dad believes everyone deserves to have someone on their side, someone to help them evaluate their decisions and make the difficult choices to prepare for their retirement.

My Dad's commitment to character is the reason I want to pour everything I have — my blood, sweat and tears — into our firm. We treat our clients and their hard-earned savings the same way we would want to be treated. We treat them with honesty and integrity, and always operate with their best interests as our first and only priority.

I believe in what we do. I believe in helping people create a brighter financial future. That is the legacy I want to carry on. That is the legacy I learned from my dad.

Megan Clark
August 2017

Introduction

I grew up in the country, in the Hudson Valley, about 60 miles north of New York City.

Back then, in the late 1950s and early '60s, most kids were involved in the Boy Scouts or Girl Scouts. And because our dads were busy working to provide for the needs of the family, moms usually took on the responsibility of organizing and running both programs.

My family had four boys and one girl, so my mom kept quite busy. Still, she and another mom, Ruth, became den mothers for my Cub Scout pack. (I confess, the animal references were fitting for a bunch of energetic, excitable boys. I suspect that keeping us focused was quite a task. Somehow, we all survived.)

Dads always seemed to get more involved when there was an active project — if we were building something or if there was an outdoor event where they could bond with their son, or sons, and other boys of similar ages and interests.

One of the biggest events for young Scouts, and one that fathers always have been heavily involved in, is the Pinewood Derby. This is not to be confused with the Soap Box Derby, where Scouts build and ride in derby cars. No, the Pinewood Derby was a little more accessible: Scouts were given a block of soft pine wood, four nails for axles, plastic wheels and a weight restriction of five ounces, and charged with creating a small car to race against boys from other dens.

To say it gets competitive would be an understatement. Dads often go to extremes to make a son's car a winner. In retrospect, the racing event is probably as much or more for the men as it is for their boys.

My dad, being an engineering type, showed me all the little things I could do that would give me an edge over the kids whose cars were slapped together with a little Elmer's glue and prayer for luck. He didn't believe in hope as a strategy. It took work and attention to detail to be successful.

Every year, we competed against about 30 kids, and the final races were always close. Sometimes the electrical timing device that judged the winners had the cars in a dead tie. Thanks to my dad and his willingness to spend the extra time and effort, my car was always among the fastest.

When I was 8, a boy I didn't know had a car that was among the slowest. It was obvious whoever helped build it hadn't paid much time or attention to its construction, and it wasn't very successful. In one race, the wheels came loose, and the car slid lamely down the ramp. The boy smiled a puzzled yet unwavering smile as he collected his car.

Yet, as the night wore on and the other boys laughed each time his ugly, blockish car slid to a losing finish, his smile gradually drooped to a frown.

I must admit that I laughed too, at first. But my laughter ceased as I watched the boy's disappointment. I also saw he had no dad there to console him. His mom did her best to convince him it was okay for his car to do so poorly.

As I kept watching, I noticed there was something different about him. I wasn't sure what it was, but there was something about his eyes that looked a little glazed over, his Scout uniform was untidy, his movements uncoordinated.

I told my dad about this boy — that he hadn't won any races and that he looked a little weird. My dad, who was an empathetic man, took me to a corner of the room, away from the noise, and explained that people are sometimes born with a disease that makes their brain work a little differently ... that some people are just slower.

Dad suggested I treat the boy as I would any of the other Scouts, but to remember that the boy might not always be in control of his actions. It made no sense to me, but Dad encouraged me to introduce myself and do what I could to make the boy feel accepted and wanted.

So, I made my way over to where he stood alone with his mother. I smiled, said hi and introduced myself. He said his name was Timothy, and I asked if I could help him with his Pinewood car. He looked to his mom for approval and, with a nod of her head, we started in, talking about the car and the work Timothy and his mom had put into preparing for the race.

His speech was broken and I couldn't fully understand what he was saying. But I listened and realized Timothy didn't have a dad to help him, and he didn't understand why his car came in last place every time it went down the track. Once he showed me his car, I immediately realized why his car was so slow.

I wasn't nearly as skilled as my dad with technical things, but I did understand from observing him that there were certain basics to having a fast car. Timothy's wheels weren't attached correctly to the car, and there were no weights to bring it up to the maximum weight threshold, which would send it flying faster down the inclined track. (You know, Newton's law of gravity.)

As an 8-year-old myself, I wasn't sure how to tell him his car was a piece of junk, but I tried to explain as tactfully as a child could that maybe my dad could help make the car a winner. I took Timothy and his car over to my dad, and he invited our new acquaintance to come to our house the next evening, as long as it was okay with his mother.

It was more than okay — a tear came to her eye as she offered her thanks. She didn't know a thing about making a car from a block of wood, she said, and she was the only one her son had to help him.

I knew right then and there: We had to make Timothy's car a winner.

As planned, Timothy came over the next night, and the three of us hunkered down in my dad's workshop and tore the car apart. My dad explained every step to Timothy, going over what we were doing and why it was necessary to make the car go faster down the track. I realized as I watched Timothy soak it in that he wasn't stupid; he was actually quite intelligent. He just processed things a bit more slowly. When we were all done, he was able to tell my dad and me everything we had done and why. Most importantly, he really understood why the changes were necessary to make his car much, much faster.

My dad wrote down some instructions for Timothy and his mom to finish the car. These were mainly cosmetic; Dad thought it would make Timothy feel a sense of ownership — like he was the one who completed the car and was responsible for having it ready to race at the finals.

The big night came, and when Timothy and his mom arrived, he immediately ran to me and showed me the finished product — the smile back on his face. My dad instructed us both to get our cars ready to race by sprinkling graphite powder on the axles, reducing friction so the wheels would turn easier.

For the next several hours, it was race after race, and Timothy's car won every time. His smile went from ear to ear. His happiness was infectious. Now, all the boys — including some who had laughed at him before — crowded around Timothy and me. We had the two fastest cars of all the Scouts.

I could tell that, despite his disability, Timothy had found acceptance among the boys.

As the night wore on, it came down to the final races to determine the overall winner. And it was down to Timothy and me, best two out of three races. As race after race ended in a tie, the Scout leader finally called it; Timothy and I closed out the night, both winners, with matching trophies.

A young Rick Clark and his friend, Timothy, proudly represent their troop at the Pinewood Derby.

From that day on, Timothy was a proud member of the gang. I felt great — I think largely because my dad was so proud of me for doing what I did, forging a friendship and helping someone. That made me happier than winning the race.

As the old saying goes, "It is not whether you win or lose, but how you play the game."

I felt I had played the game the best anyone could. Timothy and I forged a firm boyhood friendship, and he looked up to me for years to come.

That experience will always stay with me. I found out that different isn't bad — and that's an important lesson for a kid.

What I didn't realize then is that I learned something else that would affect my whole path going forward.

A boy went to a derby one night and failed over and over again. Then, the same boy went to a derby on a different night and competed as a winner every time. What changed? People with experience put their knowledge to work for that boy. Having someone on his side, someone to guide him, changed everything for him.

> What changed? People with experience put their knowledge to work for that boy. Having someone on his side, someone to guide him, changed everything for him.

This became a formative experience for me, one I believe eventually led to my calling as a financial professional. For most people looking to retire, this is likely the first and the only retirement they will be planning. We know practice and experience improve our skills. In many ways, financially preparing for retirement is a skill. So how can someone who is only going through that process of preparation one time be expected to get it right? Doesn't it make sense to put someone else to work, someone who has worked through the process and minutia of retirement preparation multiple times, and using their knowledge and experience as a guide?

Now, when people come to me for help, I like to think that I'm that someone.

CHAPTER 1

What's Your Retirement IQ?

In the financial business, you quickly learn you have a major role as an educator, with an obligation to increase the financial IQ of both clients and potential clients.

For some 37 years, I've looked at studies and surveys, and I've never seen one with results that indicated a high level of understanding about planning for retirement. There are people who are exceptions, but as a general rule in this country, we don't do a very good job of teaching people about their financial future and the hard work it takes to be successful.

This isn't a terribly recent realization. Even on the tails of the Great Recession, as people were very concerned for their retirement assets, they didn't know much about how to address those concerns. A 2011 report, "Financial Literacy and Retirement Planning in the United States," prepared for the National Bureau for Economic Research, serves to underscore this. The most damning part of that report concluded that many people have failed to address the most basic retirement needs, even when their retirement was only five to 10 years away.[1]

---

[1] Annamaria Lusardi, Olivia S. Mitchell. The National Bureau of Economic Research. June 2011. "Financial Literacy and Retirement Planning in the United States." http://www.nber.org/papers/w17108. Accessed Aug. 23, 2017.

Today, we know this is still the case. A May 2017 survey from the American College of Financial Services found that most Americans are clueless about retirement planning.[2]

 Some 1,200 persons between the ages of 60 and 75, with at least $100,000 in household assets, participated in an online poll. They were asked 38 questions on matters such as life expectancy, Social Security, IRAs, life insurance, investments and more. Fewer than two in every 10 ... TWO ... had a passing grade.

For those of us in the industry, these results are hardly surprising. It's another in a long list of surveys that prove the majority of Americans aren't ready for retirement.

Among the high (or low) lights of the American College of Financial Services findings:

- Only one in four respondents had a written financial plan;
- A significant minority never had calculated how much they should accumulate to have a well-funded retirement;
- Little more than one-third (38 percent) realized that $4,000 is the most they can afford to withdraw each year from a $100,000 retirement nest egg in order for it to last 30 years;
- About half underestimated the life expectancy of someone who had reached the age of 65, suggesting that most do not realize how long their assets must last;

---

[2] The American College. May 5, 2017. "Clueless About Retirement: Americans Fail Retirement Income Quiz." http://knowledge.theamericancollege.edu/blog/clueless-about-retirement-americans-fail-retirement-income-quiz?utm_campaign=Kaiser&utm_source=Wealth%20Management&utm_medium=Custom%20Content%20June. Accessed Aug. 23, 2017.

- Only 18% of respondents knew that about 70% of people will need long-term care of some kind.

Sound financial literacy and judgment are even more crucial today than in the last century. Employer-provided pensions have been replaced by 401(k)s and IRAs, and today's retirees are on their own when it comes to securing their financial futures. The day you retire, your HR director doesn't hand you a book that tells you how to create an income plan that you cannot outlive from the 401(k) that you've been maxing out for the last 10 to 20 years.

This is a very unfortunate state we find ourselves in. The majority of the baby boomer generation is caught in the middle of a paradigm shift in the world of retirement. We find ourselves in a situation where our retirement depends on our own knowledge of finance, yet those of us outside of financial services were never taught much on the subject, let alone given specific updates on how it has changed since pensions were the way of the world.

At our presentations and seminars, we always stress that we have a guiding principle in Clark Financial Solutions' approach to its client relationships.

Our mantra is:

- Knowledge = GOOD
- Knowledge + Understanding = BETTER
- Knowledge + Understanding + Action = BEST

Basically, our role is to give you knowledge. That knowledge plus your understanding of it makes it even better. But the best-case scenario, and the one we hope to achieve, is when you combine the knowledge and understanding with your own action. That's when you bring wisdom to life.

In this case, those three elements will put you on the proper path toward a fulfilling and realistic financial planning strategy.

Our existing clients (and my children) will tell you: I won't tell you what you want to hear. But I will always, always, always tell you what you need to know. I could not sleep at night unless I knew I had done my absolute best to educate you about your unique situation.

Cookie-cutter approaches to retirement planning are doomed to fail. Each individual or couple has a different life situation, different goals, a different comfort level with risk, and a different financial structure.

I preach listening as an art and skill. Without being careful and interested listeners, our professionals at Clark Financial Solutions cannot guide you to the proper investment decisions. I believe bad listeners make for bad financial advisors. I do not allow bad listening at our company.

Our mission is pretty basic: Take the mystery out of investing for our clients. Then, we apply our "Capital Preservation First, Capital Growth Next" approach to their situation. Ultimately, we will help our clients prepare for retirement, manage risk and work to preserve their wealth in such a way that they will not outlive their resources.

Sounds simple, doesn't it? But — and it is a big BUT — there is hard work involved on both our parts.

The first work is ours. We hope the contents of this book will convince you that our integrity-based approach and more than 35 years of dedicated service in this industry will open your eyes to the benefits of having a competent financial advisor on your side. In our experience, even a one-hour consultation can transform a client's retirement outlook. That's 60 minutes designed to provide clients with years, sometimes decades, of comfort in retirement.

It is always wise to do a quick reality check about your finances, focusing on three questions:

1. What is your strategy for reliable, inflation-adjusted income throughout your retirement?
2. Do you have a plan in place to make sure that income lasts the rest of your life?
3. Is time on your side?

At Clark Financial Solutions, these are the three critical areas we address. And if someone's answer is "no" to any of the three questions, we provide solutions.

There are five basic realities that present a challenge to each of us in retirement. In no particular order, because all five are truly of vital importance:

- We are going to live longer. This is not theory, it is fact. The good news is we will have a longer life; the bad news is that we will need income that lasts as long as we do.
- Inflation cannot be avoided.
- Health care costs rise as we age. Staying alive longer means more and more money spent at the doctor's office, on prescription drugs and, quite possibly, on long-term specialized care.
- Market risk. Let's face it … losing 25% or 35% per year is NEVER a good thing. In the past 10 years, many people have experienced significant losses, some more than once.
- Taxation. Can you tell me the last time your taxes went down? Even if Congress passes legislation to decrease taxes, take a look at the national debt and tell me, are lower taxes likely to last?

Virtually all of my clients ask, "Do I have enough? Will it last? How much can I spend?" as they consider how to address their many financial challenges.

After meticulously going through our planning process, we can answer these questions. And we TEACH our clients how to create strategies for a reliable, inflation-adjusted, sustainable income. In effect, we teach our clients HOW to spend.

Really, one of the primary pieces of preparing for the financial scene of retirement is to ask yourself if you have the answers to these questions, or if you have the resources to find answers for yourself. That's why we focus so much on educating our clients — retirement income isn't something you should have a blind faith in. Instead, you should have sufficient knowledge of and confidence in the strategies that will move you toward your retirement goals. So, what's your retirement IQ?

Top Risks in Retirement:

~Longevity~

~Inflation~

~Health Care~

~Market Risk~

~Taxation~

CHAPTER 2

Income...Then and Now

I cannot recount all the changes I've seen in my 35 years in the financial industry.

One of the biggest transitions we've had to adjust to is that the three traditional pillars of retirement income have been eroding since the 1980s.

There was a day when Social Security, pension plans and personal savings provided the bedrock for your retirement. Each was strong and virtually guaranteed. And for many retirees, those pillars were pretty equally divided.

I would be remiss if I didn't tell you that today you have much more personal responsibility for your future financial security than those folks who retired 20, 30 or 40 years ago.

Social Security seems dependable, at least if you're near retirement. But you'll have to manage it wisely. When Social Security began in 1935, a 65-year-old retiree could figure on living eight to 10 more years. Today, it isn't unusual for a person to live well into his or her 90s. That means you could be retired for 30-plus years. Deciding to activate your benefits at 62 (which most people still do) could cost you tens of thousands of dollars in the long run.

That's money many can't afford to lose because, sadly, the employer pensions that past generations depended on have mostly gone away. And the tax-deferred 401(k) plans that replaced them haven't exactly lived up to the hype: Fewer and fewer companies are offering the matching contributions that originally made them so appealing.

And there are other flaws, as well. While you were accumulating funds in your 401(k), I can just about guarantee you were told that if you kept putting in money consistently for a long period of time, you'd benefit from what the industry refers to as "dollar-cost averaging": When the market is up, your share values are up; when the market is down, your consistent contributions buy more shares on the cheap to fatten up when the market rebounds.

I also suspect you were told that in retirement, you would withdraw the same way. The industry calls that "reverse dollar-cost averaging."

But — and this is a huge BUT — when you're in retirement and withdrawing money on which to live, you might also be experiencing market losses. There are two bites coming out of your retirement-fund apple rather than one. With reverse dollar-cost averaging, your losses are compounded by withdrawals.

Let's explore two different decades to illustrate how timing and sequence of returns can affect your life in retirement.

Following, you will see a side-by-side comparison of two retirees, one who left the workforce in 1997, and the other who retired in 2000.

Each retiree began with $1 million in the S&P (the Standard and Poors 500 index ... a stock market benchmark). These portfolios also reflect that each retiree is taking income, starting at $40,000 and increasing by 3 percent every year to account for inflation. Keep in mind, these two only retired THREE YEARS APART. Further, we tacked the first three years of Retiree 1's returns onto the end of Retiree 2's so that you can see — both retirees are getting the exact same returns, they just are getting them in a different order.

I am going to say this twice. Here is the first time: You CAN-NOT time the stock market.

The chart shows how the sequence of returns can impact your investments. It also illustrates how long-term market performance affects your account after retirement.

The first retiree did very well. The market and sequence worked to his advantage. Even though he started with a small first-year loss, the next nine years were positive. Even in the years later on with negative returns, the first retiree's portfolio has grown to the point that those losses aren't completely insurmountable.

The 2000 retiree did not fare so well. Starting with only three bad years in a row, even though the two retirees have the same returns, you can still see the devastation to his portfolio compared to the first retiree.

This is where market timing and the idea of sequence of returns comes into play. Sequence of returns is the idea that it's not only your returns, but WHEN they happen that affects your results. Both retirees started with the same balance. They are making the same withdrawals. They have had all of the same returns. The only difference is WHEN they experienced those returns.

Retiree 1 Portfolio Performance				
Year	Starting Balance	Income Withdrawal	Annual Return	Ending Balance
1997	$1,000,000	$40,000	20.97%	$1,161,274
1998	$1,161,274	$41,200	17.98%	$1,321,440
1999	$1,321,440	$42,436	9.89%	$1,405,498
2000	$1,405,498	$43,709	-2.93%	$1,321,861
2001	$1,321,861	$45,020	-5.95%	$1,200,843
2002	$1,200,843	$46,371	-11.42%	$1,022,655
2003	$1,022,655	$47,762	15.97%	$1,130,563
2004	$1,130,563	$49,195	5.63%	$1,142,250
2005	$1,142,250	$50,671	1.27%	$1,105,464
2006	$1,105,464	$52,191	8.40%	$1,141,790
2007	$1,141,790	$53,757	3.41%	$1,125,091
2008	$1,125,091	$55,369	-22.50%	$829,056
2009	$829,056	$57,030	14.94%	$887,382
2010	$887,382	$58,741	8.78%	$901,428
2011	$901,428	$60,504	1.64%	$854,682
2012	$854,682	$62,319	8.23%	$857,607
2013	$857,607	$64,188	15.45%	$916,017
2014	$916,017	$66,114	7.72%	$915,533
2015	$915,533	$68,097	-1.72%	$832,877
2016	$832,877	$70,140	5.28%	**$803,039**

Retiree 1 fared pretty well in the above scenario, withdrawing $40,000 per year indexed at 3 percent per year to combat inflation.

Retiree 2 Portfolio Performance				
Year	Starting Balance	Income With-drawal	Annual Return	Ending Balance
2000	$1,000,000	$40,000	-2.93%	$931,853
2001	$931,853	$41,200	-5.95%	$837,641
2002	$837,641	$42,436	-11.42%	$704,409
2003	$704,409	$43,709	15.97%	$766,200
2004	$766,200	$45,020	5.63%	$761,782
2005	$761,782	$46,371	1.27%	$724,511
2006	$724,511	$47,762	8.40%	$733,623
2007	$733,623	$49,195	3.41%	$707,740
2008	$707,740	$50,671	-22.50%	$509,242
2009	$509,242	$52,191	14.94%	$525,343
2010	$525,343	$53,757	8.78%	$513,011
2011	$513,011	$55,369	1.64%	$465,128
2012	$465,128	$57,030	8.23%	$441,701
2013	$441,701	$58,741	15.45%	$442,134
2014	$442,134	$60,504	7.72%	$411,100
2015	$411,100	$62,319	-1.72%	$342,789
2016	$342,789	$64,188	5.28%	$293,322
1997	$293,322	$66,114	20.97%	$274,845
1998	$274,845	$68,097	17.98%	$243,917
1999	$243,917	$70,140	9.89%	$190,963

Retiree 2 runs the risk of outliving their money, using the same exact index for the portfolio and the same withdrawal rate; however, this person retired three years later than Retiree 1.

To further underscore my point, let's just take a second to look at the stock market's performance in the last few decades. Someone saving for retirement would have gone from 30 years old to 60 in these market conditions. The market has a lot of trends upward—but also several steep declines.

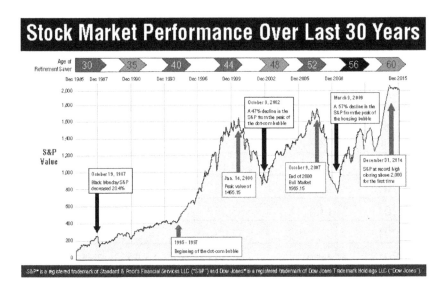

You CANNOT time the stock market. There, I said it again. Run as quickly as you can from anyone who says you can. No one can tell you with any degree of certainty what is going to happen in the market from now until 2027.

The only guarantee when it comes to the market is that it will have its ups and downs.

Do you know what happens to your portfolio when the market is up, down or sideways?

Let's pause for a little test.

- Have you been told you'll need LESS income in retirement?
- Have you been told you will spend LESS?

- Do you really wish to lower your standard of living?
- Did you work all those years to be worse off?
- Would you like a plan that takes into account what YOU want to do in retirement?
- Would you like a plan that gives you the confidence you will have enough income to live the way you wish?

Think about your answers. I suspect your responses were Yes, Yes, No, No, Yes and Yes. Good for you.

Now, let's have a serious discussion about moving from surviving in retirement to THRIVING in retirement.

It isn't an easy thing, but at some point, you'll need to take a good, long look at how much money you'll spend in retirement … and in the different phases of your retirement life.

What do I mean by phases of retirement?

Many of our clients spend more money when they first retire. We call this the "go-go" phase. There is finally time to travel, buy an RV, spoil the grandkids (as if you haven't already), pursue a hobby (sometimes hobbies can be very expensive), and on and on.

The good news? With proper planning, the "go-go" stage could last quite a while.

At some point, though — we never know quite when — most retirees slow down a bit. We call this the "slow-go" phase. You're still active, but perhaps with less travel and fewer activities. You still pursue your hobbies, just not quite as eagerly.

Finally, the "no-go" phase comes along. You spend more and more time at home. With age, you may not be able to be quite as active as the go-go or slow-go phases.

A common mistake I have seen in my 35 years as an advisor is that — again, because of poor planning — some retirees don't spend their money and enjoy themselves while they are physically able. Often they get to the no-go phase and realize the time for the go-go phase has slipped past.

Much of our company's approach to planning is found in the most wonderful and insightful quotation by the Dalai Lama. When asked what surprised him most about humanity, His Holiness said, "Man. Because he sacrifices his health in order to make money. Then he sacrifices money to recuperate his health. Then he is so anxious about the future that he does not enjoy the present. The result being that he does not live in the present or the future; he lives as if he is never going to die, and then dies having never really lived."

Don't you want to move from *surviving* in retirement to THRIVING in retirement?

This is why I am so passionate about helping retirees to not just survive, but THRIVE in retirement. Everyone has a different length of time in each phase, so your income needs for each MUST be a part of your planning.

CHAPTER 3

Risk...Your Retirement X-Factor

It's never too early or too late to put a retirement strategy in place. Whether you're 15 years out or a few months away, you'll need to shift your thinking to plan for a reliable, inflation-adjusted and sustainable income stream that will last as long as you need it to.

That plan will have to provide realistic answers to some challenging questions. We call these the "what if" questions:

- What if inflation eats up your savings?
- What if your investments lose money?
- What if you outlive your money?
- What if you have expensive medical bills?
- What if the tax code changes ... and what if it isn't to your benefit?

***

We really can't discuss future income without getting into inflation. At Clark Financial, we begin by talking about your standard of living based on your current income. Then we'll take inflation into account and have a frank discussion about growth.

That's because income can't remain stagnant. The odds that inflation will decrease — or won't somehow affect your purchasing power — well, they aren't in your favor.

If we estimate a 3 percent (and that might be low) annual increase in the inflation rate, the chart shows what it would take to maintain your standard of living.

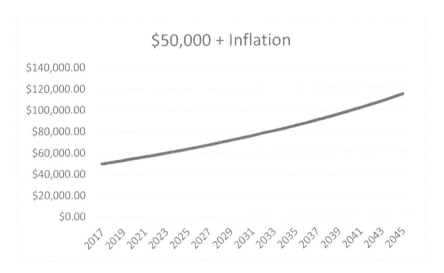

If you live on $50,000 per year today, you will need something in the neighborhood of $85,000 a year by 2035, and nearly $115,000 in 2045.

Now, apply those realities to the knowledge that your retirement savings must last a very long time.

So how do you keep up with or, better yet, stay ahead of inflation? Typically, a good approach is to have at least some portion of your assets in the market. Pound for pound, there is no other financial product that can match the potential growth of stocks. But, as shown in Chapter 2, one of the factors we face in building a successful retirement is market risk.

***

It's important that you have a strategy to put investing to good use to combat inflation, while protecting against the very real risks of market volatility.

We believe in building an all-weather portfolio, and being smart about designating which assets are best-suited to work in the market and what portion of your assets should be better situated for protection. There are some safer alternatives, including fixed index annuities, which won't lose money to a down market.

To get just a quick idea of what that can mean for you, check out this chart. Fixed index annuities can be credited value based on a stock market index's performance, but because they are not directly tied to the market, when the market performs poorly, the fixed index annuity will not get any credits, but it will not lose value because of it, either.

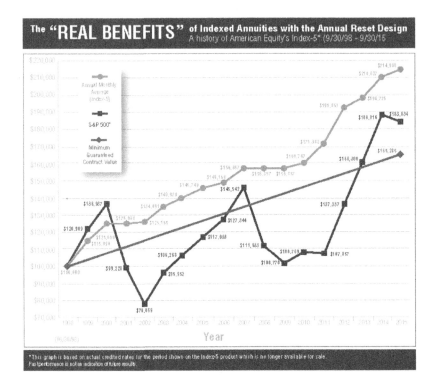

The "REAL BENEFITS" of Indexed Annuities with the Annual Reset Design
A history of American Equity's Index-5* (9/30/98 – 9/30/15)

*This graph is based on actual credited rates for the period shown on the Index-5 product which is no longer available for sale.
Past performance is not an indication of future results.

It's important to have a diversified securities portfolio that isn't weighted too heavily with any one type of fund. We also use securities investments that are not traded in the market, to truly create an all-weather portfolio.

***

Though it may seem odd to look at it that way, longevity is, indeed, another big risk we face in retirement.

A Wharton Financial Institution Center study indicates:[3]

---

[3] Ken Nuss. Dentist's Money Digest. June 23, 2017. "Create Your Own Pension Using an Economist-Recommended Method." http://www.dmdtoday.com/news/creating-your-own-pension-using-an-economist-recommended-method.

- A healthy male, age 65, has a 50 percent change of living beyond 85 and a 25 percent chance of living past 94.
- A healthy female, age 65, has a 50 percent chance of living beyond 88 and a 25 percent chance of living past 94.
- One member of a healthy couple, age 65, has a 50 percent chance of living beyond 92 and a 25 percent chance of living past 97.

Think about those numbers for just a moment. If you're 65, there is a likelihood your life will last at least 20 more years — and maybe 30 or more.

You may be retired longer than you were employed, which means your retirement savings must last a very long time.

The importance of income planning should be crystal clear to you by now.

***

As someone who has survived cancer and difficult surgeries, I am living proof of the absolute need to include health care planning in your retirement strategy.

And you can't count on Medicare to bail you out completely. According to a 2016 Fidelity report, the average couple retiring at 65 will need $260,000 to cover their health care through retirement.[4] That's a daunting number, considering that a 2016 survey found that more than half of all baby boomers have a nest egg that is $100,000 or less.[5]

If you need specialized care, and you don't have a plan for how to pay for it, it could completely blow up your savings. According to the annual Genworth Cost of Care Survey, the national median cost of a semi-private room in a nursing home in 2016 was $6,844 per month. In 2036, it is expected to increase to $12,361.[6]

There are a few different ways to help cover these costs, including health savings accounts, long-term-care insurance and life insurance policies with accelerated benefits.

I mentioned fixed index annuities just a bit earlier, and those products, which are sold through insurance companies, often have riders available at an optional cost that can give extra or accelerated long-term-care benefits.

---

[4] Fidelity. Aug. 16, 2016. "Health Care Costs for Couples in Retirement Rise to an Estimated $260,000, Fidelity Analysis Shows." https://www.fidelity.com/about-fidelity/employer-services/health-care-costs-for-couples-in-retirement-rise.

[5] Insured Retirement Institute. April 5, 2017. "IRI Baby Boomer Expectations for Retirement 2017." http://www.irionline.org/resources/resources-detail-view/iri-baby-boomer-expectations-for-retirement-2017.

[6] Genworth. 2016. "Genworth 2016 Cost of Care Survey." https://www.genworth.com/about-us/industry-expertise/cost-of-care.html.

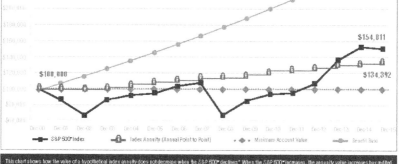

Similar to the first annuity chart I showed, the up-and-down line represents the stock market performance, while the fixed index annuity value steadily rises. In this case, the benefit base, that highest, steepest line, is also important, as it represents the potentially available benefit in case the contract holder of that annuity might become qualified to receive long-term-care benefits.

This is only one of several options available to those who are seeking to cover the cost of long-term care. We would be happy to walk you through the many options and help find the best fit for you.

***

The fifth important risk every retiree must plan around is taxation. A lot of people think they will automatically be in a lower tax bracket in retirement, but remember the go-go phase? Do you truly think you'll be spending less?

We often hear from people who decide to take money out of a tax-deferred account to pay for some kind of retirement splurge — maybe an RV or a family cruise. What's the harm, they ask; we're over 59 ½, so there's no extra penalty, right?

The problem is they're already taking regular income distributions that are now taxable. And they're getting Social Security payments — also taxable. Suddenly, they've bumped themselves into a higher tax bracket. And to get the money they need, they must take out even more to cover the taxes.

It's okay to build up your 401(k) when you're working, but in the years leading up to retirement, you should think about moving that money to a Roth or some other tax-efficient instrument, so there are no surprises when tax time rolls around. There is a general thought that in retirement we will be in a lower tax bracket.

I have two questions for you:

- Do you really want to make less money in retirement?
- Can you perfectly predict if our tax brackets in the United States will increase, decrease, or stay the same over the next 10, 20, or 30 years?

***

Once you've acknowledged the risks to your retirement, you can plan for them. That doesn't mean they won't be there, it just means you'll have a plan to avoid them and, when you can't avoid them, you will at least be in a better position to mitigate their effects on your assets and your confidence.

CHAPTER 4

It's a Perilous Journey... Don't Go It Alone

For many people, the biggest hurdle in retirement is just getting around what the word has come to mean.

After 35 years as a financial advisor, I've found that folks tend to be almost as uneasy talking about retirement as they are about saying "death," "dying" and "dead."

There seems to be an association between mortality and retirement. Seems to me people just don't like getting older. Or maybe it's because they're moving into a new and mysterious phase of their lives.

Most of us spend decades in a work environment. From our teenage years, most of us have had a job or jobs. We've had specific work hours. Company rules told us where we would work, when to arrive, when we could take breaks or have lunch, and when to go home at the end of the day. (At closing time, we "retire" for the day, but no one uses that word to describe the everyday practice of relaxing.)

During our working hours, we're reminded of the expectations placed upon us. But we mostly look forward to joining our friends and colleagues at work.

And then, all of a sudden, that day (psst ... I mean the day of our retirement) becomes a reality. We're closer to the end than the beginning.

We've paid a tremendous amount into Social Security and Medicare, but most of us don't have a clue how much. Many also deposited payroll dollars into qualified retirement plans such as 401(k)s, 403(b)s, 457s and Thrift Savings Plans. Unfortunately, we are busy earning those dollars, and the monkey falls on our back to, in addition, manage those dollars and the outcome is that we are not good stewards of that money. We are so busy living life with spouses, children and all the material things, somewhere along the line, savings were forgotten.

Until now, that is.

You, my friend, are about to embark on a new phase of life.

All the rules are going to change, especially when it comes to investing assets in a way that provides predictable, reliable, sustainable income that is adjusted for inflation. Most importantly, it must last for the rest of your life ... and your spouse's life.

> We are so busy living life with spouses, children and all the material things, somewhere along the line, savings were forgotten.
>
> Until now, that is.

And you must SHARE what you're planning — the moves you're making and why — with that spouse.

Have you ever heard the expression "If you choose not to decide, you still have made a choice?"

I often encounter what I like to think of as "self-management by default." One spouse literally goes it alone with the finances. He or she doesn't employ a financial professional and almost always leaves the spouse in the dark about what he or she is doing.

Now, if the family member who's the money manager is decently versed in finances, this might seem to make sense. But let me tell you why it's likely a setup for heartache.

I often hear from women and men who are concerned because they feel unprepared for retirement. Usually, they've never met with a financial professional and they want to know if what's going on outside their control is right or prudent.

The thing is, if it was prudent — indeed, if it subscribed to the "Prudent Man Rule" — they wouldn't be in my office having that conversation!

What do I mean by the Prudent Man Rule? It's based on common law, stemming from the court case of Harvard College vs. Amory in 1830s Massachusetts.

The rule directs trustees "to observe how men of prudence, discretion and intelligence handle their own affairs, not in regard to speculation, but in regard to the permanent disposition of their funds, considering the probable income, as well as the probable safety of the capital to be invested."

Those factors include the needs of the beneficiaries, the need to preserve the estate and the amount and regularity of income.

The Prudent Man Rule continues to be the prevailing statute in a small number of states, in particular with regard to investments permitted by mutually chartered institutions, such as savings banks and insurance companies. The rule was last revised in 1959 to imply that the fiduciary should perform due diligence to ensure the investment meets the needs of the investors.[7]

In lay terms, the rule states that due diligence should be used when diversifying a portfolio, always considering risk and preservation of assets.

And I can tell you that self-managers — again, this group is largely men — usually don't consider how important this is for a surviving spouse. Because no matter how capable he is, if he dies first — and his wife has no education or experience in the investment world — she is likely at risk.

Left to make sense of something she doesn't understand, she sees it only as a giant mess that must be cleared up. This in turn makes her susceptible to financial professionals who believe that surely everyone understands the risk side of investments, so it's fine to do whatever they see fit.

Too often, that's when I enter the picture: The widow can't sleep at night because she knows something is wrong — she just doesn't know what.

She brings all her paperwork for me to sort through, so I can make a sound recommendation for her future. I walk her through her investments, showing her what will generate income and so on. Perhaps we will focus on legacy planning. Everything depends on the needs and goals she explains.

---

[7] Wikipedia. "Prudent Man Rule." https://en.wikipedia.org/wiki/Prudent _man_rule. See also the Massachusetts Supreme Court ruling in Harvard College and Massachusetts General v. Francis Amory.

I pride myself on listening. It doesn't matter how many degrees or designations an advisor has if he or she hasn't perfected the art of listening.

I cannot count the number of times I've seen this play out. Working with widows who are deeply grieving and who don't know where their assets are and how much they have, or how their estate is situated for when they pass on, themselves… it's somewhat of a standard part of my job.

Not that I mind these scenarios; I love helping people. But I can't help but ask myself: What if more people recognized the perils of self-management — not just for themselves, but for the people they love? What if more couples pursued planning together, instead of leaving one half of a lifelong partnership to go it alone?

CHAPTER 5

Who Is Your Guide?

This chapter could have several different titles.

"Who is your guide?" is a question that is relevant to everyone who is planning for retirement. But it seems like there are a few other sub-topics that are wrapped up in that. Topics that could be reflected by titles like:

- "Here's Why You Need an Independent Financial Advisor"
- "Wall Street Hates You! Here's Why"
- "Why Does the Financial Industry Treat Retirees So Unfairly?"

And so on and so forth.

By and large Americans born between 1946 and 1964, the baby boomers, have been grossly mistreated by Wall Street and the big insurance companies — mostly because we were not educated in the workings of the financial markets.

Back when our parents were making their way in the world, the average working class American transacted his or her financial matters at the nearest savings and loan. Most people were not involved with investing in the financial markets until the last 20 to 25 years.

Which means baby boomers weren't immersed in the ways of the financial industry until we were well into middle age. This

doesn't make us stupid, but it does, unfortunately, make us igno-
rant about investing ... and who to trust.

We are still, in many ways, following the methods our parents
and grandparents used in handling their money. (Even though
we've seen that, many times, they left behind a horrible mess.) I
have been in the financial business for 37 years, and on an almost
daily basis I see portfolios that are full of volatility.

If you've ever watched the news (or looked at your statements)
and muttered, "Wall Street and the companies that sell insurance
don't care about me — they're just in it for the money," you're
mostly right. It's a business.

And, unfortunately, the way certain companies or professionals do business often can be misleading.

Most of the people who work for those companies are what's
referred to as "captive" brokers or agents. The products they sell
are limited by their employers and, as salespeople, their loyalty is
to the company — and the company's stockholders — not to you,
the buyer. It's an inherent conflict of interest.

I have been against this mistreatment of consumers for more
than 20 years. It's why so many investors began turning to independent financial advisors for help — and why it's so important to
understand and protect what that term actually means.

**

I started in the insurance business in 1980, with Massachusetts
Mutual Life Insurance Company, or MassMutual. I must tell you
upfront that I never wanted to sell life insurance. I didn't understand it, and my initial impression was that it was a less-than-ad-
mirable profession.

But the general agent (the chief executive officer of an insurance agency) caught me at just the right time and assured me I
didn't have to sell any life insurance if I didn't care to. Instead, I

started selling disability insurance, which I did see a need for. After all, anyone could have an accident or debilitating illness that could threaten their job and income, and there'd be doctor bills that had to be paid on top of their regular expenses. I dedicated myself to my job, and at the end of my first year, I was recognized as the company's No. 1 new agent nationwide.

Eventually, I did see a real need for life insurance, and became a large proponent of that solution as well.

At some point, a political event within "Mother Mass" sent us all to New England Life, where I repeated my exemplary sales of life and disability insurance. But then came a rude awakening.

I realized these giant insurance companies deliberately kept blinders on me for the first six years, so I wouldn't see what the financial markets had to offer as an independent agent. I felt betrayed. As I climbed up the ladder, I realized that, though the firms were large, the solutions they offered their customers were limited. I saw the only way to get my clients all the best products available to meet their goals was to be able to deal with all the companies and all the different offerings that encompass the universe of financial products. I decided to branch out on my own, where no one could tell me what to sell or how much I needed to sell of a certain product. That way, I could give the best of the best to my clients. It's the concept on which our

As I climbed up the ladder, I realized that, though the firms were large, the solutions they offered their customers were limited.

company was founded, and it's what we've continued to strive for since 1987.

There is no one company that provides all the best products to meet your financial goals. It's that simple. So why would you work with an agent who works as a captive? You shouldn't! As the term "captive" implies, his/her hands are tied; they can't have your best interests at heart.

And yet, people continue to work with captive agents and brokers who still use a model called Modern Portfolio Theory as the basis for investing their clients' hard-earned dollars. Why? Because we have been brainwashed by these giant companies with unlimited marketing dollars to entice you, the consumer.

 As for Modern Portfolio Theory, it was introduced in 1952. Is that modern anymore? Not quite, when you consider that today, a smartphone has replaced a computer of 10,000 times its size. Then we have Wall Street, where most of the trades are handled electronically, by computer programs. Trades are done at thousands per second. But Wall Street companies still tout Modern Portfolio Theory as the model form of investing. Something seems very wrong with that concept.

Now, what does an independent professional do that is so drastically different? We have use of all the tools that are available to design a holistic retirement plan, which reduces volatility while creating a more sustainable income.

In our financial education workshops, we always make sure we explain complex financial matters in a way that helps everyone understand the concept, irrespective of an attendee's current financial literacy. During the workshop, we display a picture of a mechanic's tool box, "The Big Red Tool Box." The tool box is 5 feet, 6 inches tall and full of all the different tools a mechanic might use to repair a car. People may think they've entered the wrong presentation at this point so, in order to clarify, the narrative goes something like this:

Here we have a tool box and supposc we had an old car sitting here in the middle of the room and it's broken. Let's say that is a 1968 Mustang, and it is cherry red just like our tool box. Like I said, it's broken. So please help me out here, what tool will we get from the tool box to fix the car? I ask the audience to help figure out what tool a mechanic might retrieve to fix the problem from the tool box. People respond with answers such as a wrench, or a socket wrench, and some even say a hammer. I normally joke with them using an old mechanic's advice, "If it doesn't work, get a bigger hammer." (Meaning we might have to beat the car until something miraculously starts working.) Wait a second, though. We don't know which tool to choose because we haven't defined or diagnosed what is broken on our cherry-red Mustang. In order to find the right tool for the job, we have to define the job.

All financial professionals have multiple drawers in their tool boxes, which hold different strategies and solutions that can be used to help a client achieve their goals. The problem lies in two main unfortunate realities.

1. Sometimes financial professionals only have access to one or two of the drawers in the toolbox and therefore give you a biased opinion about your finances when you go to them. It's not necessarily their fault; it's just a reality that stems from the fact that they either are an employee of a large publicly traded company or that they may not have all the licensing necessary to give you holistic, nonbiased advice. These financial professionals are given quotas and told what to sell. This is a very large conflict of interest, which is <u>not</u> in our clients' best interest. (I know; I used to work for them!)

2. If a financial professional is not upheld to the fiduciary standard by the licensing and therefore ethics of their firm, that person can recommend one solution over another because it compensates them with a larger paycheck.

Clark Financial on the other hand, because we are an INDEPENDENT firm, gives our clients access to all of the tools in the toolbox. We are also a FIDUCIARY firm, which means the only people we answer to are our clients, and we must always act in their best interests.Hold on, the toolbox is a good analogy, but it's certainly more of a guy thing.

Let's try a different analogy that might make more sense to the gals. Let's say you're hosting a dinner party, and you want to try a new recipe that calls for a spice you've never heard of. This spice will give the entrée a flavor that you've never experienced. You go to your local market and they have hundreds of spices, but they don't have the specific spice you need to make this exquisitely flavorful dish for your guests. The manager of the market says he's heard of the spice you need, but the store doesn't carry it because it's so rare.

So you go home and google the name of the spice. And you learn that it's available, but big stores won't carry it because the distributor won't pay them to put the spice on their shelves.

What's the point? The point is that captive agents with companies such as Fidelity on the securities side or MetLife on the insurance side all have large red tool boxes with specialty tools or, in this analogy, stores full of spices, yet they don't allow their agents and brokers to sell all of them because some options have no ongoing fees, or the ongoing fees are not high enough for them to make much of a profit. It's all about the fees!

While we baby boomers may have been navigating the financial world in near-blindness, our resistance to Wall Street's greedy, outdated model has resulted in the rise of independent financial advisors. Soon, I foresee a downward trend in mutual funds, with their hidden fees that rob you of your rates of return. I also see the decline of large wirehouses, such as Fidelity and Merrill Lynch. Independent advisors are the way of the future.

***

Managed money is also an area of great improvement and innovation in recent years.

In 2006, Congress passed the Pension Protection Act, giving consumers the ability to use Registered Investment Advisors. These advisors work in a glass box, so to speak. They do not talk to the public. They do not spend money on advertising. They rely on independent advisors to bring investors directly to them, and they are not controlled by the emotions of the market. They don't use traditional asset allocation models, because most models are archaic. Instead, they use many different investment vehicles, including non-correlated assets, such as non-publicly-traded real estate investment trusts.

Prior to 2006, an investor would have needed $5 million for each account to have access to these Registered Investment Advisors, and the average fee was approximately 10 percent. After the Pension Protection Act legislation was passed, multiple investors were able to pool money and have it invested as though they had $5 million of their own. It also made an endowment model available for the average investor at the same cost as traditional investing. A win-win situation for consumers. These endowment models have been used by Harvard, Yale and many other educational institutions across United States and worldwide for the last 25 years. The institutions collect donations from alumni and use the earnings to pay teachers and professors. They employ brilliant individuals with a background in economics, many of whom come from Wall Street. And they do not use Modern Portfolio Theory to invest their funds.

These models must produce a predictable, reliable, sustainable and inflation-adjusted income with reduced volatility. And over the last 25 years, they consistently have had returns of 10 percent or more after all fees.

This is what is required for your retirement plan as well. Though we cannot use the specialists who work for the Harvard endowment or other large institutions for our retirements, our portfolio managers mirror the endowment models. Only independent advisors such as Clark Financial Solutions have access to these types of portfolio managers.

Baby boomers have long been fed retirement advice like "set up a diversified portfolio with an asset allocation of mostly mutual funds, and then buy and hold." We call that buy and hope. That worked back in the '80s and '90s. It doesn't work anymore — and it hasn't since 2000.

It's hard to make changes to the investing philosophies that were so ingrained in all of us. The first step is to make sure the person or company you work with has a philosophy of being independent. Let me repeat that: Independent! That means you must give up all those advisors who work for a giant wirehouse or an insurance company. Conflict of interest is inherent with these types of institutions. Remember: Their stockholders come before their clients.

You should be first on the list when it comes to building a retirement income plan. When our clients call, they get an actual person working in our office on the phone 95 percent of the time. The other 5 percent, we are probably helping someone else!

***

In 2010, the Department of Labor began developing a rule to protect people preparing for retirement by limiting advice that was sales-oriented. Although the rule has been pushed back and delayed several times, it began to take effect this year. It isn't expected to be fully in force until mid-2019, but it is particularly important and impactful for those who are within about 10 to 15 years of retirement.

This new DOL rule is called, rather anticlimactically, the "Fiduciary Rule."

So, for starters, let's define the fiduciary standard and why it is important. In the financial services arena, there are two standards, the fiduciary standard and the suitability standard. Financial professionals held to the suitability standard (brokers and insurance salespeople, for example) must sell products they know a client can afford and that are in line with whatever the client's stated goals are. That's not nothing, right?

But the fiduciary standard is a cut higher. Under the fiduciary standard, a financial advisor must act in the "best interest" of a consumer. That means recommending products that are not only affordable, but the absolute best for the consumer.

For a little bit of history, in 1974, Congress enacted a very important law called "ERISA" (Employment Retirement Income Security Act). Wow, that's a mouthful. This law was part of sweeping legislation of the time, legislation that included 401(k)s and other popular savings plans, like 403(b)s, 457s, IRAs and the government's TSPs. It was Congress's attempt to help Americans save for retirement using tax incentives. It also defined what investment advisors could do — and, more importantly, could not do — in communications with people in retirement plans. While many, myself included, were in favor of these reforms, in some ways they didn't go far enough.

While ERISA clarified what the fiduciary standard was meant to be, it did not fully make it a law that all investment firms and advisors had to adhere to. While all must comply with the suitability standard, the DOL's Fiduciary Rule would make it the responsibility of the investment house, brokers and investment advisors to provide guidance that is always 100 percent in the best interest of the client when it comes to retirement planning. Let me add, the rule only pertains to your actual retirement accounts. Meaning that any IRAs etc. will be affected, but your non-qualified or brokerage accounts will not be protected by this rule. This is definitely a point that most people we speak with are confused about.

I personally love this rule, because it could put all advisors on the same level playing field, the field on which my firm has been playing since 1987. I keep repeating my support for the rule because, while it may be a problem for 98 percent of financial professionals today, it has never been an issue for the independent financial advisor community. So, while we're a smaller "boutique" investment advisor firm and we do things outside the box, we have always been able to pull and use more tools from the toolbox. WHY would you want to work with anyone who could not give you all the tools?

While others in our industry are busy asking the government to carve out exemptions — and greet each rule delay — we here at Clark Financial are looking forward to the day all financial professionals act in the best interest of their clients.

CHAPTER 6

Plans Need Action

Each year we do all we can to arrange an in-depth visit with every single client we serve. Those meetings are often conducted in person, but we also hold them by phone, email and even the old-fashioned way, by writing and hand-mailing a complete report.

If I had my way, every meeting would be face to face. Being with the person allows us to better listen and observe. And we like to see our clients and catch up with what has been going on in their lives.

I think we have a significant number of single female clients because of this approach; we listen intently and understand what they're saying as opposed to just hearing what we want to hear. We truly care about what is important to them.

I would like to share the story of a person I'll call Dorothy, a dear client of mine. It's a prime example of how building trust over time uncovered a concern for her, and how we were able to come up with a solution that was of vital importance in her life plan.

Dorothy was born in 1939. She is a vibrant **widowed** 78-year-old retired teacher with three full-grown children and seven grandchildren who live in Virginia and New Jersey. As so many retired teachers do, she has a pension from both the county and state. She also has a tax-sheltered annuity, better known as a TSA, in which she has saved more than $100,000. In addition, she had some other non-qualified funds and even commercial property in New Jersey, and two residences, one in New Jersey and one in Reston, Virginia.

I first encountered Dorothy at a public workshop in 2006, so she's been our client for over a decade. When we had our most recent visit to review her current investments and how they were doing, the first thing that came up beside her TSA and non-qualified funds was the issue of long-term care.

Dorothy didn't want her children to feel responsible for her, but she would never listen to us on including long-term-care coverage in her comprehensive plan. So we had to come up with a solution. After reviewing all her different investments, I found she had an old annuity with Great American Life that was worth $94,000, which she had gotten into before we met her.

We decided it was worth looking for another option that was in Dorothy's best interest. The problem was that her old annuity had something called a "rolling surrender charge" that would never go away, no matter how long she kept it.

We hoped to find a newer product, one that came with a bonus big enough to offset the cost of the surrender charge and, if necessary, that would pay extra should she need long-term care. And we found an American Equity contract with a 10 percent bonus. It wasn't enough to fully offset the surrender charge, but Dorothy opted for a rider that would grow, or "roll up," at 7 percent annually, guaranteed, in six years, even after taking required minimum distributions (since this annuity was held in an IRA). So, $94,000 would turn into $120,000 for retirement income purposes.

This was a substantial increase, or, as I would call it, an arbitrage — trading in one contract that would always have a surrender charge for one that would increase the value to Dorothy by more than $24,000.

The other consideration in this whole picture is that Dorothy got very concerned when she didn't have a considerable amount of savings. Her goal was to have at least $100,000 in liquid savings, which I believe was far more than she needed, but this was what made her comfortable. She had $56,800 in a Capital One savings account earning less than 1 percent interest, and she had $120,000 in a credit union account earning a quarter of 1 percent. To add to it, she had an indexed annuity with Fidelity and Guarantee that I set up years ago, which was out of surrender, meaning she could do anything she would like with that contract. It was accumulating only 3 percent in interest every year at that point, so I suggested she take $40,000 from the savings accounts and add that to the Fidelity annuity contract (which would bring the contract to a total of $108,000).

She felt very comfortable having that much liquidity, so I then suggested we take the balance of the money from savings and add it to the American Equity contract with a special rider that grew at 7 percent for income purposes. While she couldn't take it as a lump sum, the overall point of this exercise was to give Dorothy more income in a few years and the assurance that, should she need long-term care, the annuity contract would double its payments to her for up to five years. She also had another contract called a  Secure Income Annuity, which had an initial premium of $120,000, a lifetime income benefit rider of 7 percent and a health-care doubler that doubles her income if she should need it for long-term care.

When all was said and done, Dorothy would be able to increase her annual income by $20,661 or, if she needed long-term care, $41,322. Adding in her pension of $91,000, Dorothy would have a total benefit of $132,003. This was all in addition to what we call her risk-based assets. Those investments included money that was invested in the stock market, through directly held stocks or ETFs, and investments in private companies. Many of those private investments were registered with the SEC and had a prospectus, however, they were not traded in the stock market and therefore were not directly correlated to the volatility of the stock market.

We can think through the nitty gritty details, follow complex strategies, analyze potential outcomes and come up with an excellent approach to managing the risks inherent in retirement. But if a client doesn't decide to pull the trigger on all this planning, it is just so much ink on so much paper.

Dorothy was ecstatic to say the least. She was so glad she took the time for this visit so we could create a much-needed benefit for her and increase her savings rate of return to 3 percent.

There's just one problem: Dorothy relied heavily on the opinion of her son, who lived in New Jersey.

I suggested I write all of this up for him to read, and I said I would be more than happy to call and explain the plan and its benefits. But Dorothy, who liked her independence, insisted she would handle it.

Months went by, and Dorothy still didn't get a chance to sit down with her son and explain the plan we engineered. Obviously, when there are a lot of changes to a plan that is currently in place, it takes a good bit of understanding. With the time that has elapsed, I expect I will have to start all over, talking her through it the next time she's in the office.

Unfortunately this is a pretty common scenario. We can think through the nitty gritty details, follow complex strategies, analyze potential outcomes and come up with an excellent approach to managing the risks inherent in retirement. But if a client doesn't decide to pull the trigger on all this planning, it is just so much ink on so much paper.

This is one of the problems advisors encounter just about every day. You can lead a horse to water but you can't make it drink, as the old saying goes. Because Dorothy has been a client for so long, I know she takes a good amount of time to think things through before she puts them in place. I just hope for her sake that she doesn't procrastinate too long. She's losing money … and time.

CHAPTER 7

Finding the Silver Lining of Your Dark Cloud

All of us have gone through disappointments in our lives. Winners are separated from losers by how we react and whether we turn those disappointments into positives. I know this for a fact. Allow me to share how two huge disappointments impacted my life and how I used them to create a silver lining each time.

The biggest disappointment of my life was learning I would never be able to pursue my dream career path.

If you read the introduction, you may recall the significant effect being a Boy Scout and growing up near Stewart Air Force Base had on my life. (If you didn't read the introduction, you should!) As time and life progressed, I leveled up from Pinewood Derbies to Soap Box Derbies, Klondike Derbies and all the other things Scouting involves: camping out, wilderness programs, etc. These in turn led me to Search and Rescue, or, as it was called back then, the Civil Air Patrol.

I was fortunate enough to be introduced to a United Airlines pilot who was a bachelor, and a Scout in his youth. Jack owned his own airplane and was heavily involved with Scouts. His plane was an old tail-dragger, I believe it was a 1942 Yankee Clipper. We hit it off right away, and by the time I was 15, I was learning to fly with Jack in the Civil Air Patrol.

To say I was interested in becoming a pilot was an understatement. I practically breathed aeronautics at that age; by the time I turned 16, I already had taken the ground school courses and, on my 17th birthday, the "legal" age to obtain a pilot's license, I took my private check ride (the equivalent of an automobile driving test). And I passed! Of course, this led to a bit of an ironic situation. In New York State at that time, the legal age for a driver's license was 18. I had my pilot's license for a year before I earned my driver's license.

For years, I flew with Jack in the Civil Air Patrol. It was an incredibly formative period in my life; during the time I was in Civil Air Patrol, we actually found two lost hikers and one downed aircraft. As you can imagine, these experiences practically poured kerosene on the fire of my passion for flight.

The years flew by and, before I knew it, it was 1971 and I was off to Embry Riddle Aeronautical Institute in Daytona Beach, Florida, to further pursue the love of my life: FLYING.

I'd saved my money for 10 years in hopes that it would be enough to get me through my early college years and training so I could move to the next step: enlisting in the U.S. Air Force pilot training school. I had $18,000. That might not seem like much today, but remember, this was 1971.

The plan was simple. ("It's real simple" is a term I've always used as motivation to complete a task.) I would receive an instrument rating, a multi-engine rating and a commercial ticket. A "ticket" is aviation lingo for a license. Then I would apply for "fighter pilot school" in one of the branches of the military. The Air Force was my first choice, but either the Army or Navy would have been more than adequate. It just had to be a fighter pilot school. After my military service, I would move to take the next step toward my dream career: a pilot with one of the many commercial airlines.

One evening while flying with my instructor, he asked the control tower to do a "radio out" approach. This meant someone in the tower would flash different colored lights at our plane, signaling instructions for landing. Normally, this is for emergency landings only — it's to be sure you can communicate with the control tower even if a storm or freak accident interferes with radio communication. There are three colored lights: white, green and red. The tower shoots the lights just as you would with Morse code; however, it involves sight rather than sound.

When the lights were shot at me, I was to tell my instructor their meaning. Since I was a very dedicated student of flying, he was shocked when I got them wrong. He asked the tower to repeat them. Then he asked me the difference between green and white.

I was confused about what this might mean to my dream career, but I knew it couldn't be good when he said I needed to take a color blindness test, or, as it is called in the aviation world, a test for night blindness.

I learned I was red/green colorblind. More significantly, I learned my dream of flying as a military or commercial pilot was OVER. Yes… OVER.

Pilots who suffer color blindness are restricted to flying during daylight hours; they cannot become instrument rated and they cannot obtain a commercial pilot's license. This was my "dark cloud." But since you aren't reading this book to find out about obtaining flying licenses and experience, I will move quickly to "the silver lining."

I tell this story so you can understand that I have had a dream shattered and was forced to move forward. My great disappointment led me to a new career path, which has ultimately guided me to you and our other great clients. I believe my bitter defeat led to a better life for all of us.

The clients of Clark Financial Solutions and our ability to help them secure a comfortable retirement has become my silver lining.

Almost from birth, my parents and grandparents taught me the value of family. On a daily basis, I saw the sacrifices they made for me and my four siblings. Clearly, that message rubbed off on me. I feel their influence as I go about the business of helping our firm's clients with their financial planning and goal achievement.

My daughter says I'm a people pleaser. I stand guilty as charged. There are countless stories about how we have helped clients, but a few really stand out.

Kelly is a country girl from West Virginia. When we met, she had recently divorced her husband, a developer in northern Virginia. His company had declared bankruptcy, but Kelly was awarded some $2 million prior to that.

The real problem was that she had signed several loans with her now ex-husband, and the banks were coming after her $2 million. Sadly, before we met, the banks had forced her to relinquish part of the money. She was left with only $1.2 million.

I contacted my attorney, and we devised a plan to preserve the balance of her assets. We mortgaged her existing home to the max with a value of more than $1 million. Then we sent her to Florida, where she purchased a house in Del Ray Beach for about $200,000 cash. Kelly took what was left (about $1 million) and placed it in an annuity with a little company called Life USA. That was 1999.

In the state of Florida, two things can't be taken from you: your home and any money you have in annuities. We said GOTCHA! to the big bad banks.

Today, that little company has become Allianz Life Insurance Company of North America. Kelly is still a Clark client. Her $1 million annuity is now with American Equity and has a net worth of $2.4 million. She sold her Del Ray Beach house for a nice $180,000 profit and moved back to her original home in Virginia.

She paid off the entire mortgage and lives off the interest on her $2.4 million. And she won't make a major purchase without our talking about it first. Over the years, such is her faith in us, she also has referred some $12 million in assets to Clark Financial Services, through various friends, family and colleagues who needed guidance.

My other true story is about Sarah.

About seven years ago, our mutual friend, Janet, introduced us. Janet is Sarah's best friend and a stockbroker at a large wirehouse. Before the introduction, Janet called and gave me a very long explanation as to why she wanted me to take care of Sarah.

Sarah was divorced and working as an executive assistant to the president of a local company where she participated in an Employee Stock Ownership Program (ESOP). About a year from retirement, Sarah had three terrible fears. She was terrified of losing money, of running out of money and/or being forced to rely on her daughters in the event of long-term health care needs in her later years.

Knowing all that, Janet told Sarah that she was not the best choice possible to help her and that I would be a much better fit. Janet knew I conducted my business with preservation of capital as my first priority, and that I was prepared to work with Sarah on her two other fears.

Sarah was a sweetheart and very detail-oriented.

Our first meeting lasted two hours (my absolute upper limit on focus). Over the next year we met numerous times. My objective was to fully educate Sarah as to the process and the many things that needed to be considered in a plan that would meet all her needs as well as the ever-present issues of taxes and inflation.

We went over the different phases of how she would receive her ESOP money, spread over four years and totaling about $1 million. Keep in mind that Sarah had never dealt with this volume of money, and, of all her company's ESOP participants, including her boss, she was receiving the largest amount of money.

Sarah was very hands-on with her retirement money and wanted to know how each financial investment worked and fit into her picture.

Let me fully explain how we approached Sarah's situation and how, with our three-step process, we were able to develop a specific plan that met her financial goals while considering risk factors, lifetime income needs, long-term care and the legacy planning she intends for her two girls.

It begins with the first step, which is vision. Vision is about what you

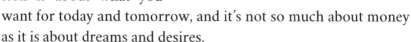

> Vision is about what you want for today and tomorrow, and it's not so much about money as it is about dreams and desires.

want for today and tomorrow, and it's not so much about money as it is about dreams and desires.

I will not breach Sarah's privacy and our pledge to confidentiality by going into detail about all her goals, but in our first of many meetings, we determined that she wanted and needed income.

She did not want to be dependent on her two daughters later in life. And, she wanted to be able to help her children now and in her legacy planning. Deep down, there were more items on her wish list, but those were the basics.

Next, we moved to the discovery phase. This is the meeting where we get to the naked truth about assets — how she felt about them, where her investments were focused and their respective levels of performance vs. risk.

We also wanted to know whether she was with another financial advisory firm. If yes, what was the relationship and how long had she been a client? Was she happy? Would we be stepping on toes if we suggested moving her assets to Clark Financial to obtain the solutions she would need for today and the future?

Finally, we wanted to make sure she had enough trust and confidence in us to know we were the last financial planner she would need for her life and that of her children.

After we gathered all the needed information, we developed a plan with a starting point she completely understood. All questions are always thoroughly addressed in our process. We started with the basics: protecting her assets and establishing an income stream to satisfy her immediate needs with guarantees.

Next, we gave her the picture from 30,000 feet, as Megan likes to say, about how we intended to build a plan that meets her goals. We designed a legacy plan for her two daughters by using a 10-year paying life insurance policy with absolute guarantees. In another meeting, we educated her about investments in real assets that are not traded, in order to avoid market volatility. It took months for her to feel comfortable with investments that paid her 5-9 percent distributions in hopes of yielding total rates of return in the 10 to 12 percent annual range.

Most Americans have never heard of some of these types of financial vehicles because Wall Street will not make them a part of your portfolio. They don't have ongoing fees to the advisors, which means there is less profit for Wall Street brokers. We help

Clark Financial clients keep more money by getting rid of unnecessary fees.

As you may have surmised, we are very much outside the box. We hear the same question often: "How come I haven't heard about this before?"

Once they know about these options, people are much more trusting of us and our way of doing business.

It took the better part of a year before Sarah was completely comfortable with the total plan. But today, she is content with the totality of her portfolio and enjoys an average rate of return of 7 percent after fees in a very volatile market.

Any person who knows anything about the market is ecstatic with a 7 percent rate of return.

At every step, we built trust. She has become a good friend, a part of the Clark Financial family, and a raving fan who has brought us many referrals. Her belief and trust in us has allowed us to build our client base and make even more friends. Funny how that works. There is gold in them thar hills, and don't forget the silver that got you there.

Clients like Sarah become great advocates for Clark Financial, referring numerous prospects to us. We meet with Sarah on a quarterly basis to review, update and make any changes necessary to balance and maximize her holdings. With Megan as a fully licensed advisor, we have a legacy that should last for decades, looking out for the needs of Sarah and her daughters.

I like to think we took Kelly and Sarah's dark clouds and helped them find their silver lining.

There's another old saying you've probably heard, "Any port in a storm." And it's true that these two fine women could have sought help — and found it — with many financial professionals.

But I believe it's a testament to Clark Financial that we can still say, years later, that they trust us to find strategies to keep them comfortable in retirement. Whenever our clients come to us with a question or concern, we're there to help with thoughtful and innovative solutions.

CHAPTER 8

Are You Ready to Collect

There are two major stages in our lives when it comes to the way we handle our assets: the accumulation phase and the distribution phase.

During the accumulation phase, you build wealth and resources to provide an income source for yourself in retirement. You grow your portfolio, but you don't tap into it.

In the distribution phase, the money you saved provides income for your day-to-day expenses and to live the lifestyle you dreamed of all those years while you were working.

Each of these financial phases can be affected by a number of circumstances, some we can control and others we cannot, including the law, government programs, the environment, politics and social changes.

Let's talk about the accumulation phase first, since this is presumably the longer of the two and critical to the health and safety of the nest egg we're building for later.

Most of today's more recent or soon-to-be retirees were raised by the Greatest Generation. This generation is defined by two segments: the G.I. Generation (Americans born from 1901 to 1924), and the Silent Generation (born from 1925 to 1945). They taught us that if we worked hard and saved on a regular basis, we would be able to have a successful adulthood, with success measured by financial as well as social growth.

Our baby boomer generation, those born between the years of 1946 and 1964, grew up in a time of great challenges and exponential growth. We experienced everything from Woodstock to space exploration to the advent of the internet. This is the generation I am mainly referring to in this chapter, because this is the generation that is ready to collect.

I was born in 1950 and from the time I was about 8 years old, I worked hard, had many different jobs and learned a slew of skills. I could devote an entire chapter to the jobs I had by the time I was ready to enter college. I was willing to do almost anything to make and save money; the desire to be successful led me to save and acquire assets to keep up with the Joneses and Smiths.

Life was good for most in my generation during the accumulation phase. If we wanted it, we set our minds to it and acquired it. We accumulated things: big houses, boats, second homes. But — and this is a big BUT — were we ready to enter the second phase of life, the distribution phase?

Unfortunately, the baby boomers were so caught up in the now that many of us failed to plan well enough for the future. Some of us even had our retirement benefits change halfway through our careers. In place of the pensions our parents and grandparents had and could rely on, today's pre-retirees largely have invested in qualified retirement plans such as IRAs, 401(k)s, 403(b)s and 457s (the last are for government employees). In addition to qualified plans and annuities, government employees often have Thrift Savings Plans.

All of these plans are valuable benefits and can be good ways for people to save for retirement. Unfortunately, people often are so busy with their jobs and their lives that they don't take the time to learn about all the options. They just go with whatever investments are offered by their employer's plan, and take on too much volatility in a buy-and-hold position. I like to call it the buy-and-hope position: You hope it will come back after periods like 2000 and 2008, when the market dropped 30 percent to 50 percent. This type of asset allocation was developed in 1952 and called "Modern Portfolio Theory." The theory doesn't work anymore and, I am sure you will agree, is not modern. Think about the stock market even in the 80s. If you wanted to buy shares of Coca-Cola or IBM, you called your broker and told him what you wanted to do, he then walked over the ticker tape that was printing out in the office to tell you the share cost, and how much you  needed to invest. He would then write up a trade ticket and someone on the trading floor would get that trade placed for you. The trade took at least 15 minutes and probably closer to an hour to get accomplished. Things have changed and the way we invest needs to change with it.

We could spend hours talking about this theory and why it doesn't work. What's more important, however, is that baby boomers and pre-retirees have put their hard-earned money into these tax-deferred retirement plans for the last 20 years.

These plans are regulated by the government, and Uncle Sam sets the limits on how much employees can deposit on an annual basis. While they have improved these plans in recent years, they still have not educated consumers on a more formal basis. Which is why it's vitally important that boomers and other pre-retirees take the initiative to understand what the future will look like when they need to use their invested savings for income.

If you understand the basics, you will see in the following chart that, in the last 100 years of charting tax rates, taxes are at the lowest level they have been in 100 years. So, taxes really are on sale right now.

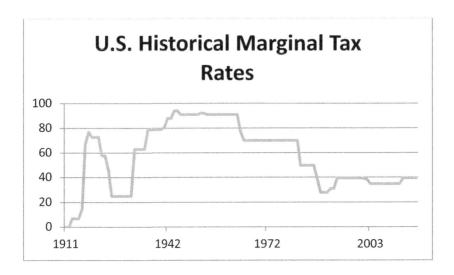

I would bet that 95 percent of consumers have *never* seen a chart like this that displays the historical tax brackets. What does this mean to you and me? It's important to understand that taxes have only one way to go, and that is up. When tax brackets go up to pay back the massive amount of debt the government has amassed, using the most tax-efficient products will be the best way to help reduce your tax liability.

A perspective we hear from many of our prospective clients is that they will be in a lower tax bracket in retirement. This could be true for some people. However, for most of us this is most likely not going to be the case. Let me explain. As we age, and continue to make more as we get into our higher earning years, we somehow wind up spending more. We buy nicer, newer cars, and perhaps buy a bigger house, or go on bigger vacations. Then by the time we are 65 or 70 we are accustomed to a certain way of life and just because we retire does not mean that we will want to reduce that standard of living.

To add insult to injury, all of that money that we've worked so hard to save into our IRAs or 401(k)s becomes a mandatory source of taxable income at 70 ½ years old. What does this mean? It means the amount we withdraw from our tax-deferred accounts once deferral ends will most likely not only affect how much of our Social Security gets taxed but will affect how much we have to pay for our Medicare premium, also.

This means Roth 401(k)s are the only way, from a tax perspective, to invest in retirement plans.

The majority of prospective clients we meet with do not have any type of written income plan...That is not good enough.

And for those already in retirement, bleeding down IRAs through Roth conversions will be the most efficient way to take distributions. Especially when taking distributions in excess of required minimum distributions (RMDs). Every case and client is different, sometimes with time not on our side these strategies may not make sense, however I urge you to work with an advisor who can walk you through all of the pros and cons of them.

This is only the tip of the iceberg when it comes to tax planning. We are not CPAs, and we urge you to see your tax planner (not just a tax preparer!) to get a complete picture of what's available. As independent financial professionals, our firm can work with your tax professional to create a strategy that will help keep your hard-earned savings in your pocket.

The majority of prospective clients we meet with do not have any type of written income plan. They will tell us their advisor told them they can withdraw 2 percent or 4 percent of their portfolio and they should be fine. That is not good enough for our clients. No one wants to be 90 years old and not be able to afford their groceries. This is a reality…and one we need as a nation to start working on fixing now. Some people are living longer in retirement than the total number of years they spent working. Having a written income plan with some sort of contractually guaranteed income as a piece of it is necessary for survival.

CHAPTER 9

Wills and Trusts

I left this topic for the end of the book because it is an area of financial planning that most people don't like to think about.

Why do people put off making a will? I've been having this discussion with clients for 40 years, and I've heard all kinds of excuses … none valid.

For most, procrastination is simply a better option than considering the end of one's life. Very few of us wish to face our own mortality. But you must think of your loved ones. Not having a will upon your death (dying intestate) adds another layer of stress at a terrible, emotional time.

I keep a current copy of my will and trust in the office. Showing clients my up-to-date estate planning documents is my way of saying, "See, I'm not asking you to do anything I haven't already done for myself and my heirs."

The simple act of showing my will can start a fruitful discussion, and clients often immediately follow through with getting their own.

If you are an advisor reading this, I urge you to complete your own will and have it available to prove to those you work with that you practice what you preach.

These days, you can construct a will in a matter of minutes for a ridiculously low cost on a variety of valid legal websites. These "template" wills might not always be perfect for your situation, but they are far superior to having no will at all.

To use an attorney is your choice; to begin the process today is your obligation. Take. That. First. Step.

In 2016, the media was in a feeding frenzy over the realization that pop icon Prince hadn't left a will. People came out of the woodwork like termites, claiming all kinds of tenuous family ties and hoping to get a share of his fortune. Since he died intestate, the crazy cycle of who should take over and who would get what began its dizzying spin.

All could have been avoided with a visit to an attorney.

With all the wise professionals you would imagine worked for Prince, it boggles the mind that one or more of them didn't insist the estate be protected and preserved through proper planning. To me, and this is just one fellow's opinion, it is inconceivable.

Back to the issue at hand. Let's start with a question. What, exactly, is a will?

As defined by Wikipedia, it is a legal document by which a person (testator) expresses his or her wishes as to how property is to be distributed after death. The will also names the executor who will manage the estate. And there is devolution of property by inheritance. Documents such as wills go back to the Roman Empire. (If it was good enough for Julius Caesar, it should be good enough for you.)

A critical point to remember is that only the original will is acceptable to probate court. Once you have completed the document, make sure you keep it in a safe and secure place and that your executor knows where to find it. Photocopies do not count. Let me repeat: *Photocopies do not count.*

Now, allow me a confession. There was a time when I was guilty of irresponsibility in a specific area, I had grown children who believed they were too young to need a will.

Then I realized: What if my kids have their own children and some terrible event occurred? What if both parents died?

Beyond the tragedy of their deaths, there would be no plan in place for raising the children. What if the rest of the family disagreed with how we, as grandparents, would raise them?

Don't be naïve. It does happen. We hope and pray it won't, but it does.

Can you imagine the heartbreak — perhaps after spending thousands of dollars finding a solution as to who should or should not raise the surviving children — of having a judge or the court system tell you that someone else would do a better job?

In your heart, you would know the parents wanted you to raise their kids if there were a tragedy, but there is no document to prove it. Because there is no will, your world (and perhaps that of the kids) would fall apart.

All because someone didn't take an hour and spend a few hundred dollars.

While making your own will, make sure your adult children are doing the same. Be smart and help your kids be smart.

Moving on.

Wills have many important uses. A prime example is that a will allows the deceased to identify certain assets intended for specific beneficiaries. Having a will helps stop the squabbles about who should get Grandpa's favorite shotgun or Grandmother's most prized necklace. Families have been torn apart over a set of dishes.

A will that clearly states who should receive what, while it may be disappointing to some, leaves specific directions from the deceased and provides a necessary measure of certainty.

I won't even get started on how much this helps when a person has children from a previous marriage to consider in addition to a surviving spouse.

Family feuds have started over a pocket knife, book collection or riding mower. Please do not allow that to be your legacy.

I will share a very personal and painful story with you. It happened in my family and it was awful. But it helps explain clearly why we should recognize the need for planning ahead using wills and trusts.

In the early 1990s, I was able to aid my parents in doing some very necessary planning.

Family feuds have started over a pocket knife, book collection or riding mower. Please do not allow that to be your legacy.

When my dad retired at age 65 from his lifelong job as an electrician at the Hudson River power plant in New York State's Hudson Valley, he had to make a serious decision about how to take his pension.

Since financial advice is my profession, he asked my advice, and we decided he should choose the option known as "life only." It meant he would get the maximum amount of money each month, but when he died, the checks would go away; there would be no survivor benefits.

There was a logical reason for making this choice. Fifteen years prior, when she was about 50, my mom decided to go back into the workforce. She had raised five children who were now out of the house and it seemed a good time to earn extra money. She began work at a local school cafeteria.

One winter day, as she was leaving her workplace, she slipped on the ice and ruptured a disc in her lower spine. She was taken to the hospital and surgery was performed immediately.

I remember it as if it were yesterday.

It was a Friday and a huge snowstorm was forecast for the weekend. The doctor, whose name I do not recall, was in a hurry; he wanted to escape the storm by getting on the last plane out of town to Florida.

Tragically, he did not take the necessary precautions in prepping my mom for her surgery. As a result, she contracted a staph infection in her spine.

Remember, this was in the '90s and we did not have all the antibiotics available today. So, the staph infection spread up her spine, leaving her with degenerative spine disease.

As I recall, over the next few years, she had at least six open-back operations with six fusions, a metal cage around her spine and morphine drips to ease the pain.

Why have I given you all this background? Because her situation led everyone in our family to believe she would die well before my dad. She had endured multiple painful surgeries and her quality of life wasn't good.

So, Dad chose the "life only" option for his pension, thinking it would give them more money for their lifetime.

But my mom was Tough with a capital "T" and fought to live. When my dad was diagnosed with Parkinson's at age 75, everything in their world changed. Yet, the pension choice had been made and there was no going back.

In 2007, my dad died from complications of Parkinson's, and my mom was left with Social Security and her worker's compensation as her only meager sources of income. And I do mean meager.

Being from the Greatest Generation, my folks were very private about their financial affairs. If you've dealt with aging parents, you know exactly what I mean. But in the planning I was able to do for my mom — after we knew the full details of her money situation — we took her house, which had no mortgage, and placed the title in an irrevocable trust, with two trustees and several successor trustees. The rest of the assets had been placed into a revocable trust earlier on in their estate planning while my father was still alive.

This decision in itself was an issue, as some siblings were made trustees and others were not. These decisions are always tough ones, and parents make these decisions for various reasons. Oftentimes our clients desire for an independent trustee to be put in place rather than one or several of their children, or sometimes they don't have children. This trust planning allowed our mother to claim Medicaid if she needed to, and no entity could take the house. (Medicaid's spend-down rules state that a person must use all their personal assets before becoming eligible for the benefits of the program.)

It was not supposed to work this way, but life happens. You must be able to change plans on the fly.

After the money ran out, it fell to me to foot the bill for everything not covered by Mom's Social Security, Medicaid and workers comp. Luckily, I've been able to put myself in a situation where this was not detrimental to my future; however, it was still a burden, financially, physically and mentally.

Thank the good Lord for my youngest daughter, Megan, who stepped up to handle administration of the bills … and there were a ton of them … as well as joining with my son, RJ, to help physically. As I was in Virginia while Mom was still in New York, those kids were a blessing. I shall be forever grateful.

My eldest, Carrie Anne, was in Denver expecting a child (grandson Hudson), so she was unable to have a physical presence. She helped Megan and RJ as best she could, but Megan did the heaviest of the lifting for her grandmother.

This is probably why Megan, now my partner in the firm, is so committed to helping everyone she can with their retirement planning. She is devoted to helping folks like her grandparents avoid the "what ifs" of life.

Flashback 20 years: When doing their planning, my parents made me and my brother Michael co-trustees of their trust. It was awkward to be singled out from our other three siblings, but we knew we had to make the best of it. We tried not to take sibling implications of improper influence all that seriously and to stay above the pettiness that sometimes occurs within a family.

In the years preceding my father's death, my two younger brothers passed away from different medical challenges. Michael, the youngest, died of cancer and Mark did not survive a grand mal seizure. We miss them deeply each day.

Michael and I had always tried to be collaborative rather than dictatorial. Yet, at the conclusion of all conversations and after hearing from the interested parties, you MUST follow the instructions and wishes laid out by the grantor of the trust.

In a will, it is the testator who expresses his or her specific wishes as to how property will be distributed at time of death. The grantor is trust terminology for the person creating the trust. That person decides what property is to be included and who the beneficiaries will be. This is my segue to trusts.

Ahhh, trusts.

The major difference between a will and a trust is that the will is executed at death, while a trust can be activated while the grantor is alive.

Another big distinction is that a trust escapes probate, unlike a will, and can significantly save on costs.

So, I suspect you are asking, why should I/we have a trust?

A few years back I was visiting with one of my favorite estate planning attorneys. The question came up and he said people had a trust for primarily one of two reasons:

1. To save money by escaping probate; and

2. They didn't have complete faith the designated person would carry out the wishes made by the grantor.

At first, it seemed funny. Then I realized the deep truth within his statement.

Suppose a beneficiary was a spendthrift or a person with special needs? Now, it's not so funny.

It is a tough situation when a child or grandchild needs to be given direction, and even tougher when that person possesses zero or limited ability to exercise discretion over certain assets.

It reminds me of one of my dad's favorite sayings: "Must Do is a tough master."

So it is with being the trustee of a trust. The task at hand can be challenging, but you must fight through the difficulties and master the task.

There are many types of trusts. Most trusts for estate planning purposes are revocable. Irrevocable trusts, generally speaking, are used when the grantor wishes to remove assets from estate taxes.

The matter of taxes on estates can be a bit of a moving target, so make sure you stay informed. In 2010, estate taxes were repealed. The following year, estate taxes were reestablished, but with a limit of $5 million. That figure increases every year as it is adjusted for inflation and only 0.2 percent of estates will face a tax liability due to the new limit. However, any president has the ability to change that. So staying on top of that will ensure your estate plan is executed as you desire.

It's common to see a trust tied to a pour-over will. In plain terms, this means that, at the time of the testator's/grantor's death, anything that was missed in the will "pours over" into the trust in order to provide probate protection.

My opinion? Every person should have an estate planning attorney produce a proper will and a trust. It will save your loved ones thousands of dollars that might otherwise end up in probate court. Some of our clients want to spend every last dollar that they've worked their lives to earn. And that, my friends, is perfectly okay. I had a client tell me one time they want the last check they write to be to the funeral home, and they want it to bounce! We had a good laugh about that one together. However, the reality of the matter is that we cannot predict our future. Accidents happen, and life is taken away from some sooner than one could imagine. Estate planning is an important part of legacy planning, whether you want to create one or not. I'm assuming if something were to happen to you, you would want your hard-earned money given to the people or charities you care about most, and not to Uncle Sam.

I'm assuming if something were to happen to you, you would want your hard-earned money given to the people or charities you care about most, and not to Uncle Sam.

Your financial advisor can and should be an important part of this process, which also could include your tax professional. Making it a team effort will ensure all your bases are covered. And if there are any questions from family members, you'll be able to confidently stand your ground.

I'm proud of the legacy I've created already, and know it will continue to thrive for decades to come. What legacy am I referencing? I'm referencing Clark Financial Solutions, and everything that we stand for. I'm also talking about my wonderful daughter Carrie, and her love for working with children with severe autism. I'm talking about my brilliant son RJ, who can climb any rock you put in front of him. I'm talking about my grandchildren, Hudson, and Colette, and any more I am blessed with in the future. Family is a huge part of who I am, and I want them to be provided for as best I can, even when I'm no longer able to walk on this earth. Hopefully, with Megan running the show at Clark Financial, this legacy will be able to continue on well beyond my own timeline.

CHAPTER 10

Legacy

BY MEGAN CLARK

I often hear from my peers that I'm young to be in the financial services business, or that I have a lot to learn.

I agree there is always more to learn. I hope a day never goes by in my whole life that I do not learn something new.

But a load of letters behind someone's name or even multiple master's degrees won't necessarily mean he's a better advisor. What really matters is that your financial professional is truly doing the best job possible for you and charging you the least amount of fees necessary.

I mean, does it matter how many certifications someone has if he's working in his own best interest instead of yours?

In this business, accreditations seem to come and go in significance. Over the years, I watched my father work so hard to achieve this designation or that, only to find that in five years or so, it was no longer relevant. For example, a very popular accreditation right now is the RICP, or Retirement Income Certified Professional. But who knows what will be the next big thing to have?

What I do know is that, thanks to a shift in our society that put the burden of securing one's financial future onto the individual, people are realizing they need a sustainable income plan. So, my goal is to keep learning how to best serve my clients in that way. I currently hold my Series 63, 65 and 7 securities certifications, my life and health insurance licenses (as well as long-term care) and I am pursuing my CERTIFIED FINANCIAL PLANNER™ designation. It is a two-year program, with a lengthy exam at the end.

I hope you read Chapter 7, about my dad's eternal optimism and the importance of being able to find a silver lining when dark clouds roll over your dreams. Let me take a second to tell you about my own silver lining experience.

My lifelong dream included playing collegiate soccer before ultimately devoting myself to a career of helping people … as a doctor. The journey to my graduation gave me a perspective on life that many young people do not get the chance to acquire. My father was diagnosed with Stage 4 cancer in my senior year of high school, which made rounding out my straight-A high school career challenging. I found it difficult to sleep most nights; instead I wanted to sit by his bed and take comfort from listening to his breathing. I spent countless hours driving to and from Johns Hopkins Hospital.

When life throws you a curve like that, you tend to revise your priorities, and for me, school went on the back burner. My teachers were very gracious and let me do as much extra credit as they could, but it was just too much of a hit to my grades to attend my top school, James Madison University, where I had a scholarship to play soccer. Instead, I went to Virginia Wesleyan on an academic scholarship. Despite everything, I started every game freshman year and held my own with many assists and a game-winning goal.

Midway through the season, I collided with an opponent and tore two muscles in my quadriceps completely in half. Soccer was officially over for me. After licking my wounds, I followed my dad's oft-repeated advice to get back up and brush it off, and I decided to focus solely on school.

I made a new goal of transferring into the best school in the state, which also happens to be one of the best public schools academically in the nation. I graduated from the University of Virginia in 2008 and, after a short stint with a large corporation, decided to help my father with marketing at his financial advisory firm for a year.

Now, more than 10 years later, I'm a fully licensed advisor and love what we are doing here for our clients.

Being a small, family-owned independent financial advisory firm is not always easy. In the David and Goliath analogy, we are certainly David; we simply don't have the funding to compete with giants such as Morgan Stanley, Smith Barney or Raymond James in our marketing campaigns.

But, what we can do is change the industry. I believe this. As a small independent family firm, we can allow the clients to be our boss. We're able to do the best job possible for them because we don't have a CEO saying which products we should be pushing. We don't have shareholders to please. The only things that matter are our clients' needs, goals and successes.

Every time I face a disappointment or a frustration, I think of my dad telling me, "Get up, you are fine!" He would then say, "Learn from it and move on."

I definitely apply his lessons to work hard and play hard in my business. There is always more to learn, another important project looming or improvement needed in a certain area. It's easy to find yourself working 12 hours a day, six days a week. I have to remind myself to create my own balance … working really hard but always remembering to go get some exercise or eat dinner with friends. The balance keeps us as advisors more grounded, and also lessens the chance of burnout.

I'm humbled by the trust my clients have in me, and I never want to take it lightly. After all, many of them have worked years to acquire their assets, and they deserve to know they'll be taken care of for their lifetimes, and that their legacies can be preserved for their beneficiaries.

In much the same way, one problem that arises for any small business is that of a legacy, or succession plan, as we'd call it in the business world. This is a concern for many retirees who work with independent financial advisors, because who wants to be in the middle of retirement only to have your financial professional drop out of the game, sell the business or dissolve their holdings?

That's why you should make sure the person you're working with has a plan in place for the future.

At Clark Financial Solutions, we plan to keep the succession in the family. Since my dad is in the business of helping people to and through retirement, he, of course, spends some time thinking about his own plans. As he looked around, he saw that many advisors choose to sell their book of business to the highest bidder when they're ready to retire. After spending his lifetime working

on behalf of his clients and their families, some of them for generations, he wasn't satisfied with the thought of handing them off to just anyone and not having a say in how their accounts were managed down the road.

Instead, he put his work into designing a 10-year succession plan. When an assisting advisor has worked at the firm for 10 years, he or she will have the option to begin buying shares of the firm, becoming a part owner. Yes, I'm Rick's youngest daughter, and I've worked at the firm for 10 years ... I think you see where this is going. I have spent the better part of the last decade preparing to fill some very big shoes. This way, my dad knows his wishes and desires for upholding the integrity of the business will be carried on.

What started as a dark cloud turned to a silver lining and now has become my life's work. My original dream was always to help people, and that help is needed for today's retirees more than ever.

The financial world is an ever-evolving industry; it changes every single day.

The financial world is an ever-evolving industry; it changes every single day as new legislation is passed, new investments are dreamed up, and new people influence our country's economy.

Hopefully, we are headed toward a more consumer-focused industry, where the days of fly-by-night product pushers are limited. Right now, of course, there are still too many people who claim to be advisors but who are truly salespeople promoting whatever products give them the biggest paycheck.

Many of the changes in the industry are due to cultural and generational differences, as well. The Greatest Generation, survivors of the Great Depression and extreme savers, have largely passed their inheritance to the baby boomers, who are on the verge of transferring their wealth to their children.

I have to say, though there are exceptions, I don't see my millennial counterparts saving at least 10 percent of their earnings. Instead, I see social media posts of lavish vacations, luxury vehicles and houses with gourmet kitchens (though most meals are not cooked or eaten there). Unfortunately, I fear our world of instant gratification (thanks, internet) has led to a collection of debt for my generation.

I've encountered this same spendthrift philosophy among many of our boomer and Generation X clients. When we're evaluating their savings, many bring up an anticipated inheritance as something to factor into their savings goals. To me, this is not financial planning. That is what we call basing our livelihoods on hope and, as a fiduciary, that isn't good enough for me.

My fiduciary responsibility — my responsibility to act in the very best interests of my client — leads me to give hard advice in these circumstances.

Another place I feel called to offer some hard advice? Before I wrap things up, I'd like to call all my fellow ladies to the floor.

Women have made impressive strides when it comes to personal finance. According to the U.S. Bureau of Labor Statistics, in households where both spouses work, nearly one-third of women out-earn their husbands. Women now control almost 40 percent of investable assets in the U.S.[8] But when it comes to saving for retirement, women continue to lag behind both in their preparedness and the value of their savings. Nearly three-quarters of women have never created a financial plan for retirement and, on average, women's retirement accounts are nearly 40 percent less valuable than the accounts of men.

Of course, there are many different reasons why this is happening, but I want it to change! Far too often in our office, we meet with widows who were never educated about what their husbands were doing with the family finances. Did you know that today the

---

[8] American Funds. March 6, 2017. "Women Control A Growing Percentage of Investable Assets." https://www.americanfunds.com/individual/news/by-the-numbers/women-and-money.html.

average age of a widow in the U.S. is only 59 years old?[9] No matter who is in charge of the finances in the family, all parties need to be educated about how to handle the money. It's not okay to be grieving your loved one's loss while at the same time trying to figure out how you're going to pay next month's bills.

I want to change the way women deal with the family finances. I want all of us to be educated enough to be involved.

Of course, for anyone, the best place to start is knowing the right questions. Whenever you are vetting an advisor, you need to find out three things:

1. Who does that advisor work for? The answer should be you, the client. You want someone with an independent firm and not an employee of a large company.
2. Are they held to a fiduciary standard? The answer should be an immediate yes. If it isn't, run!
3. Are they giving you holistic advice? Are they talking about estate planning and taxes and referring you to the appropriate professional who can assist you? Many advisors know exactly what they are going to recommend before you even walk through their door. That is not holistic advice.

Women also need to recognize that we live longer than men. We're more likely to need long-term care, and for a longer period of time. Traditional long-term-care insurance isn't necessarily the best option. Did you know you can purchase a life insurance policy that also will cover you if you need it for long-term care? This

[9] Amy Florian. Financial Advisor. July 11, 2013. "Serving Widowed Clients Whatever Their Age." https://www.fa-mag.com/news/serving-widowed-clients-whatever-their-age-14829.html.

gets rid of the whole "if you don't use it you lose it" scenario of traditional long-term-care insurance.

There are better ways for us to plan than to just simply hope we don't get sick.

Whether you are a man or woman, old or young, I'd like to share one of my favorite quotes:

"In the long run, we shape our lives and we shape ourselves. The process never ends until we die. And the choices we make are ultimately our own responsibility."
Eleanor Roosevelt

Sometimes, particularly with regard to our finances, we feel helpless — as if we cannot change our own lives. Take heart! As Mrs. Roosevelt said, the choices we make are ultimately our own responsibility. Let's educate ourselves and empower ourselves to make better financial decisions.

Together, we can change the world.

Megan Clark

ACKNOWLEDGMENTS

A project of this magnitude doesn't get finished without plenty of hands on deck. As it is primarily an extension of myself and the work that I have done, I'd like to take a moment to thank the people who have been most important in making me who I am today. I'd like to thank my parents for raising me to know what real ethics are. I'd like to thank my early mentors who helped me learn the ins and outs of this industry, which in turn paid out untold fruits. Thank you to my family for their unending support in this and all endeavors. To my children, Carrie, RJ and Megan, thanks for always believing in me. And, last but not least, thank you so much to all past and present (and future!) team members of Clark Financial who help make our company all that it is.

R ick Clark is the founder and president of Clark Financial. He has more than 35 years of experience in the financial industry and holds a business degree from James Madison University.

While working at a large firm after college, Rick yearned for a firm that truly catered to his client's needs. This developed into a vision of owning a business that focused solely on providing honest, simple financial advice for people of all ages. Clark Financial was founded in 1987 and our advisors will help you create a customized investment and income plan.

Rick was nominated as a Top Five Advisor of the year in 2011 by Senior Market Advisor Magazine. Rick has raised a family of three accomplished children, and is a cancer survivor. His vision of guiding our clients toward a Brighter Financial Future continues to be the foundation of our firm.

Two roads diverged in a wood and I — I took the one less traveled by, and that has made all the difference.

—ROBERT FROST

Megan, a graduate of the University of Virginia, is the CEO of our firm, as well as a wealth manager and Rick's daughter. She grew up learning about the business and fell in the love with the fact that our clients truly are the boss. Her passion to help others is fulfilled with every client we support. She is a Retirement Income Certified Professional and is currently working towards her Certified Financial Planner (CFP) certificate. When Rick decided to "retire", he knew Clark Financial would be in good hands. Megan was born and raised here and currently lives in Reston with her husband James. When she's not helping people create a Brighter Financial Future, she is either playing with their new puppy Chloe, spending time staying fit, or volunteering with local organizations.

A customer is the most important visitor on our premises, he is not dependent on us. We are dependent on him. He is not an interruption in our work. He is the purpose of it. He is not an outsider in our business. He is part of it. We are not doing him a favor by serving him. He is doing us a favor by giving us an opportunity to do so.

—MAHATMA GANDHI

W e hope that, while the products and strategies we've covered won't necessarily apply to you and your circumstance, this book has given you some food for thought. Hopefully, the stories herein will get the wheels turning about your own circumstances, your own plans and who you are trusting with your financial future.

If you would like a review of your current plans and strategies, or if you have any questions about the topics of this book, please contact us at Clark Financial Planning:

Ph: 703.796.0957| F: 703.796.0838

1984 Isaac Newton Sq. West, Ste. 203

Reston, VA 20190

www.clarkfinancialplanning.com

clientservice@clarkfinancialplanning.com

Made in the USA
Middletown, DE
14 August 2020

15364014R00060